Childchurch

Homily Outlines for Preaching to Children

Ronald B. Mierzwa

Resource Publications, Inc.
San Jose, California

Editorial director: Nick Wagner
Prepress Manager: Elizabeth J. Asborno

Reprint Department
Resource Publications, Inc.
160 E. Virginia Street #290
San Jose, CA 95112-5876

Library of Congress Cataloging in Publication Data
    Childchurch : homily outlines for preaching to children /
Ronald B. Mierzwa.
        p.   cm.
    Includes bibliographical information and indexes.
    ISBN 0-89390-370-1 (pbk.)
        1. Children's sermons. 2. Children's mass. I. Title.
BX1756.Z9M54   1996
251—dc20   95-52994

Printed in the United States of America

00 99 98 97 96 l 5 4 3 2 1

*Ronald B. Mierzwa's "ChildChurch" logo, which appears with
various modifications on the front cover, spine, title page, and
each chapter title page in this book, is a registered trademark.*

This book is lovingly dedicated to my godchildren:

Leigh Ann Colbert
  and her brother, Kevin,
Robin Leigh Santarini
  and her brother, Ryan,
  and her sisters, Lynn and Devon,
Darcie Leigh DeMers,
Jason Patrick Kolpack
  and his brother, Ryan,
and Katie Rose Burke,

who generously shared their wondrous world
of childhood with me.

Contents

Acknowledgments

I gratefully acknowledge the following people, who, by their interest, concern, and support have sustained CHILDCHURCH throughout the years: Rev. John Kasper, OSFS; Beth Lenegan, Alan Lukas, and Carol Corey, my fellow travelers on the CHILDCHURCH odyssey; the children of the parishes of Our Lady Help of Christians Chapel, Cheektowaga; St. Mark's Church, Buffalo; and St. Lawrence Church, Buffalo, who challenged me to preach the Gospel in new and creative ways.

Introduction

Although the *Directory for Masses with Children* (DMC) ascribes great importance to the role of homilies in children's celebrations (48), proposes that they be dialogic in nature, and gives revolutionary permission for the homily to be given by someone more familiar with working with children than the presider (24), very little attention has been devoted to the *homily* in children's celebrations. Numerous books and aids have been published on the planning of children's liturgies, but the homily is often the most neglected dimension of their formats.

As an educator, presider, and friend of children, I have experienced the critical importance of the homily in any children's celebrations and liturgies. The "Introduction to the *Lectionary for Masses With Children*" (LMC) echoes this vital concern: "Because the explanation of the Scripture readings is so important at Masses with children, a homily should always be given" (10). Of all the areas where input and planning are concerned, the homily is often the crux, the focus, the prism through which all the other elements can blend, combine, and rise to vivid expression. So many children's liturgies and celebrations have flown—or not—because of the presider's treatment of the homily. Sometimes the homily is the most dismal segment of an otherwise thoughtfully planned and prepared celebration.

This sad state of affairs has many origins: a lack of collaborative effort (though assistance might be offered and available), little or no input from children themselves, a casual attitude toward children's needs and prayer, a lack of comfortableness with children, a well-worn presidential style that is inappropriate for children, and so on—many other excuses can be found. There may also exist a well-founded reluctance to propose a non-ordained preacher for a celebration after a thoughtful reflection on and honest evaluation of a priest's gifts, capacities, and liabilities in preaching to children. It may prove difficult (if not futile) to try to dislodge a pastor from officiating and preaching at a children's assembly of worship when he feels a pastoral compulsion to do so (e.g., at a first communion, school graduation, etc.).

However, the DMC is quite clear that, with the proper permission of the pastor or rector of the church, an adult who is participating in the celebration "may speak to the children after the gospel" (24), offering a reflection on the Scriptures. This permission is reiterated in the recently issued *Lectionary for Masses With Children* in its introduction, paragraph 10. The publication and use of this lectionary gives added importance to the church's desire that children be gathered in worship so that "together...in the Spirit we may listen to and respond to the word of God in Christ" (1). The LMC also gives added impetus to the mandate to assist children in conforming "their lives to the message of the Scriptures that they have heard" (2), a mandate that particularly emphasizes the role of good homilies at children's celebrations.

With the increasing trend in the church to conduct separate Liturgies of the Word with children and to worship with assemblies of children specifically, there are now broader opportunities offered for an adult other than a priest to preside and, obviously, to preach at these assemblies of worship. Since a homily is an integral part of any celebration of God's Word (DMC 48), it can be presented by a qualified baptized adult who has the inclination, training, and experience to do so, in conjunction with the ordained ministers of that particular church.

Before continuing on the theory and theology of children's homilies, I need to make some initial observations. I define "children" as youngsters between the ages of three or four (pre-school) and fourteen years of age (junior high school level). The Good News is for all ages, but appropriate acknowledgment of age factors— attention span, cognitive development, affective skills, life experience, etc.—can effectively aid the planning team, presider, and preacher in composing children's celebrations. The assembly of children demands much attention and serious prayer and thought, especially by those concerned with its catechetical and liturgical formation.

Also, my comments presuppose the value and need for good children's liturgies, the worth and dignity of children, and the seriousness of this endeavor. Children are capable of worship; they can pray and do pray well; they are already experimenting with reflection (though they need guidance); they are gifted with the Spirit; and, obviously, they belong in the community of faith. It is their right by their very baptism into the church.

These comments (and homilies) arise from my personal experience and are addressed to those worship occasions (liturgies and prayer celebrations) when children comprise the bulk of the assembly.

Finally, I anticipate that those engaged in children's liturgies are both theologically and liturgically responsible, see their involvement as an expression of their own spirituality and faith, and are able and willing to share sound and prayerful experiences with our children.

The purpose of this introduction is to address the issue of children's homilies *with* and *for* you, the preacher, whether you are ordained or not. Preaching at children's celebrations and liturgies is not quite the same as preaching at adult worship; actually, it can be a more flexible, liberating, and enjoyable experience!

A pressing need for preachers in children's liturgies is to cultivate *friendships* with children. Most priests in particular do not have many friends who are children. Ease with and familiarity with children can only come with exposure to and involvement with children and their world; it takes time and energy, yes, but it is invaluable. The world of children is a constantly shifting kaleidoscope of heroes, rock stars, television programs and movies, toy fads, school events, family occurrences, peer pressures and activities, and sports; at times children even speak a language of their own.

Gaining entry into this world offers any adult unique insights into the concerns, differences, and dynamics of childhood. There need not be any loss of adult integrity when adults enjoy children.

The benefits of such contact are many: an increased comfort level in working with children, an ability to draw upon significant children's issues, a chance to weave vibrant and interesting images into their homilies, and an opportunity to offer Christian perspectives on matters that touch their lives. Spending time with children can also awaken in you a greater sense of wonder and awe, of enthusiasm and excitement, of child-like appreciation for creation and people.

The more comfortable you feel with children, and the deeper the rapport you develop with them, the greater ease you will feel in discussing, enjoying, and moving among them. You may even enjoy a personal freedom to move out of the pulpit, as an obvious example, into and among your young assemblies. This freedom in turn enables the children to draw closer to you and also have increased contact with the images that the homily proposes.

This familiarity with children also enhances your ability to develop gestures, postures, and actions in harmony with the ages of the children and local usage (DMC 33).

In no way must this insistence on a relationship between children and preacher be interpreted as a demand that you become childish; the gift to be cherished is child-*like* faith and trust. Thus, in speaking and working with children, childish language, jargon, and behavior is inappropriate for adults; it may well be detrimental for the task at hand. You share in their world, and in a well-crafted homily, the sharing is reciprocal: the adult world, the child world, God's world.

This need to be familiar and comfortable with your children's world(s) invites collaboration with parents, teachers, coordinators, and friends of children. They are precious allies in your attempts to reach your children in fresh and compelling ways; they have a variety of insights, criticisms, and proposals to put at the service of children's homilies. Reach out!

A children's homily—and, in general, all children's liturgies and celebrations (DMC 15)—focuses on provoking a greater and more informed response to the Gospel in the lives of the children; they need to experience God's story as their own. The homily needs to be specific to the ages, needs, and experiences of the children. You can assist that process by offering relevant, specific, and open-ended suggestions as to how the children can view their life experiences in the light of the Gospel.

Avoid vague generalities such as "being nice" and "helping people"; rather, suggest or evoke more concrete and practical areas where the children can exercise their own Christian call. For example, you could suggest "cooperating with the school bus driver" or "keeping your hands to yourself while standing in line," etc.

If the children offer the vague generalities themselves, you could pursue their answers to form more concrete and practical applications. Help the children to identify particular actions, behaviors, words, and attitudes in their own lives that need the compassionate and courageous vision of the message of Jesus.

Thus, a children's homily is formative of healthy Christian perspectives on a variety of situations, issues, and concerns that children (and later, as adults) experience. An integrated and well-prepared homily will bear elements of scriptural research and background, catechesis, humor, exhortation, prayer, spirituality, challenge, and practical application, resulting in a well-blended final version which is shared with the children as an opportunity to see, feel, act on, respond to, and trust the Gospel message. Strive for a sound homeostasis in the homily; combine verbal with non-verbal language, listening with doing, and child-like enthusiasm with adult guidance in your aim to involve the whole child. There is no value in trying to dictate the end result; after all, the Gospel message encompasses a multiplicity of responses, among which you offer one or two views.

A children's homily employs strong, vivid images— images that provoke, intrigue, and endure in a child's imagination. It is your privilege to attempt to make connections between life experiences and Spirit experiences and to evoke reflective thought on the way we approach life, love, relationships, and situations as Christians. Strong images carry a power of their own and plant seeds that will bear fruit in future years. The power of scriptural images is particularly strong. Scriptural imagery also cautions us against over-emphasizing any intellectual or cognitive presentations and appeal more to children's emotional and affective levels, as the DMC urges (33-36). One strong image, around which all words, gestures, and activities revolve, will have a lasting impact and value to the children.

Preachers traditionally rely heavily on the dialogic method of children's homilies, i.e., the question-and-answer version. To its credit, this method has the advantage of simplicity and ease, and it attempts to engage the children in the process, at least verbally. However, several issues immediately arise from a dependence on this approach:

1. Oftentimes the preacher's questions are obvious and possibly inane, leading to boredom and restlessness on the children's part.

2. In many cases, it soon becomes apparent that the preacher is looking for the "right" answer; those children who perceive that they gave the "wrong" answer may withdraw from the homily out of embarrassment or wounded pride.

   If this has been your approach, perhaps you can ignore the desire to maintain tight control over the "beginning, middle, and conclusion" of the homily by asking open-ended questions, making it a true dialogue, even at the risk of letting the homily develop along different lines than originally sketched. You could creatively include the children's comments into the flow of your homily and thus transform the homily into an exciting eye-opener.

   A quick review of the kind of questions that Jesus asks in the Gospels reveals a fine example of this technique of asking open-ended questions. For example, in Luke 10:26, Jesus asks, "How do *you* read it?" (my italics).

3. The preacher effectively limits other creative avenues of approaching the homiletic topic, such as mime, drama, storytelling, art, music, visual and/or audio aids, or film.

Incorporating some of these avenues can involve the children more physically in your presentation. In my experience, we have presented a number of dramatic ventures to illustrate the Gospel message (using both adult and child actors): "Martin the Cobbler," "The Juggler," and "Stone Soup" (three commercially available folk stories), "Fantasy Island" and "Noah's Ark" (my own stories), and several other playlets that demonstrate the thrust of the Gospel more effectively than any words that I could prepare. At the end of each presentation, I would conclude the experience with two or three well-honed sentences to help the children make connections, reinforce the theme, and suggest some kind of follow-up activity.

Working from a prepared text or "off-the-cuff," try to discover and develop a format that most closely fits your personality and liturgical style. Personally, I find a carefully constructed and comprehensive outline the best method, for it offers me the reassurance of focus and direction. By the time of presentation, I am so familiar with the outline that I rarely need to refer to it and can be more relaxed; I may even feel free enough to drop it if the Spirit moves all of us to do so.

Some approaches—storytelling and drama, for instance—may require more attention to the detailed progress of a story and make the written word a bit more crucial in terms of images, story progression, and verbal cues. Again, comfort comes from experimentation and familiarity.

In conclusion, there are few limits to your personal creativity and to the creativity of your liturgical resource staff, your children, your parents, and the Spirit. Fly with it!

Process

The process of creating a children's homily is the same for creating any homily, except perhaps that you have greater flexibility in the means employed. Any homily is the intersection of sacred Scripture and life.

Step One

Individually, at first, various members of your planning team (ideally composed of both adults and children) reflect on the Scripture readings for that particular celebration. Ponder, reflect, and sit with the Word in silence; let the experiences, impressions, and images percolate in prayer. Focus on the impact of the message in your own lives, how it "sounds" to you, and how you respond to it in faith.

Then, as a team, share—in faith—the meaning and message of the Scriptures from your individual experiences. Out of the creative ferment of your prayer, discussion, and analysis, a common theme gradually emerges that is pertinent and manageable as the team wrestles with the message. (Not only the homily but the entire celebration is illumined and guided by this exchange; other dimensions of the planning process take form.) A major advantage of this collective effort is that many adults and children work together to create the homily, sharing the responsibility for its implementation.

Individually and collectively in this process, then, dream the questions of the Scriptures: How do I experience this message in my life? How does it resonate in my life? How does it speak to me? What aspects are more appropriate for the age group in consideration? Here in particular, both the adult and child imagination can have free rein.

Step Two

Thorough preparation is required; late Saturday afternoon or an hour before the celebration is too late. Once you identify a focus, consider various approaches for the homily's presentation based on the assembly. Should the homily incorporate dialogue, drama, music, etc.? The homily should be simple, participatory, and direct—whatever the means. The team should research the assessment and availability of resources as well as work out the details involved to ensure a smooth- flowing presentation.

Step Three

Keep it simple, keep it brief, let it flow. Speak in words the children will understand without resorting to "baby talk" or childish language.

A simple focus, briefly explored, can easily be handled by most preachers and can guard against wandering way off track or getting too involved or complicated. A simple object or item can help maintain that focus and at the same time provide that strong image so critical in working with children.

Step Four

Maintain a positive thrust: encourage the children, affirm their efforts, praise their attempts. There is no benefit whatsoever in any kind of diatribe, veiled threats, or impatience. Indeed, there is a golden opportunity present to affirm their worth, celebrate their gifts, and raise their self-esteem as children of God.

Step Five

In your concluding remarks, suggest ways to implement the scriptural message; in other words, help the children become action-oriented. Gradually ease the children from merely hearing the Word to doing the Word. As the DMC maintains, the emphasis is to help the children "to proclaim Christ to others among their family and among their peers, by living the 'faith, that works through love' (Gal 5:6)" (55).

Step Six

Learn to let go. Every child hears what he or she needs to hear; individual children draw different applications from every message. They as children (and we as adults) are free to take an image, a concept, a dream, and filter it through their imagination as it leads them wherever and whenever they need to go. God is at work here, and God needs space to creatively move in their midst as well. There may be no tidy answers or pat formulas at the end, but that is all right.

I offer the children's homilies in this book only to stimulate your own creativity and ingenuity in working with children's liturgies and celebrations. They have all been presented at various children's liturgies, with varying degrees of appeal and impact.

I offer them as learning experiences for presiders, preachers, teachers, liturgists, and friends of children. Just like learning how to ride a bicycle (get on and do it!), the best way to experiment with children's homilies is to do them, learn what works and what does not, and gradually develop a comfortable style that fits both you and your assembly of children.

Some of these homilies may violate some of my own guiding principles (as outlined above), but they were stepping stones in my own struggle, on my own journey to communicate the Christian message; to convey enthusiasm and energy to his young disciples; and to evoke, encourage, and enjoy the power of the risen Christ.

Fly!

Advent (Anticipated Christmas)

Focus Group

General

Liturgical/Scriptural References

Fourth Week of Advent (Years I and II)

Notes

This homily is ideal for the last school Mass before the Christmas holidays. At no point, however, use the name of Jesus to identify the "new kid"; let the children figure it out.

Situating the Homily

There's a new kid on the block—he's just moving in. This new kid would love to get to know you and be your friend; in fact, that's why he's moving into the neighborhood.

Developing the Main Points

I hope you'll take the time to be his friend; he's more than willing to be friends with you.

I hope you'll show him around the neighborhood:

- include him in your games
- share your families with him
- help him out
- stick up for him
- take him along with you when you go places and do things
- talk to him often

- keep in touch

- discuss things with him

He's really interested in you. Let him know your interests; find out what he's interested in. Let him know you care about him!

Make him a big part of your life—a very big part of your life, a very important part of your life—because he cares for you.

Conclusion

There's a new kid on the block, and you have an excellent opportunity to meet him soon! His birthday is (*Monday, Tuesday, Wednesday—whenever Christmas is*).

Don't let him get run over by a reindeer!

Related Liturgical Suggestions

Carry the fourth candle for the Advent wreath in the opening procession.

All Souls

Focus Group

General

Notes

Liturgical/Scriptural References

Feast: November 2
Lectionary Series: #789-793

Situating the Homily

Today we celebrate All Souls Day. Today we remember all our friends, our grandparents, and other relatives who have died.

Developing the Main Points

Today we pray that these people

- will be with God
- will be happy
- will be taken by God into heaven, where they will be filled with joy, be filled with peace, and be in love forever.

Today we remember them with love. (Prayer is looking through the eyes of love.)

All Souls Day is:

- a day of prayer
- a day of remembering

- a day of peace
- a day of forgiveness
- a day of hope

for all those who are no longer with us, all those who have died.

Conclusion

Conclude with a moment of silence in which children close their eyes, remember their beloved deceased, and hold them gently in prayer, entrusting them to God our Father.

Related Liturgical Suggestions

With advance preparation, the children of the assembly may compile a list of deceased friends and relatives (e.g., grandparents, aunts and uncles, etc.) for inclusion in either the general intercessions or eucharistic prayer.

Apostleship

Focus Group
General

Notes

Liturgical/Scriptural References

Any feast of an apostle

Situating the Homily

Today we celebrate the feast of one (two) of Jesus' apostles, _____ (and _____).

Developing the Main Points

What/Who is an apostle?

How many apostles did Jesus have? (*No one knows for sure; we know the name of twelve, but surely there were more.*)

An apostle was a person with a

- big *heart* to love Jesus and people
- big *mouth* to tell people about Jesus and his Father
- big *hands* to do God's work

(*If appropriate, include a short biographical sketch of the specific apostle(s) being celebrated.*)

Like _____, we are all called to be apostles too!

We can use our hearts, hands, and mouths for Jesus!

Can anyone tell me how we can use

- our hearts

- our mouths

- our hands

for Jesus and the Gospel?

Conclusion

Continue to be an apostle today and every day!

Related Liturgical Suggestions

Place a picture, icon, or statue of the apostle(s) in the gathering area before the liturgy. Hand out a prayer card with a prayer by or about the apostle(s) after the liturgy.

Ash Wednesday

Focus Group   **Notes**

General

Liturgical/Scriptural References

Lectionary #220

Situating the Homily

Lent begins today. Yes, it's Lent *again*, time to "relent!" What does it mean to "relent"? "To give in."

Developing the Main Points

Lent: The time to

- give in to the Lord
- reject sin
- remember our baptismal promises
- *give in* to the Lord.

Prayer: Listen more closely to God's Word in our lives.

Almsgiving: Practice works of charity

Fasting: Cut down on food.

- Stop stuffing ourselves with (junk) food and fill ourselves with the rich food of the Gospel.
- Give in to the Lord.
- Give up sinful actions and attitudes.

- Give more of our time, energy, resources (money).

Lent: Time to reconnect to our baptism, when we promised to keep God's commandments by loving God and our neighbor.

Lent: Time to repent, to "turn around" our lives and get back on track"back to the Lord.

Ashes signify our sorrow for having wandered away from the Lord; ashes symbolize our desire to relent, reconnect, repent, return to the Gospel

Lent: Time to give/give up

Lent: Time for lenten exercises

Conclusion

Stop and think: What do you need to do—what can you do—to get back to your baptismal promises, to the Lord?

(Silence)

Stop. Think. Then do!

Repent: Turn your life around.

Reconnect: to your baptism.

Return: to God's way of living.

Relent: Give in to the Lord!

Related Liturgical Suggestions

In the homily, suggest a lenten fast (e.g., Rice Bowl meal) in which all the families in the parish might participate in addition to individual fasts.

Baptism of the Lord

Focus Group

General

Notes

Liturgical/Scriptural References

Sunday after January 6
Lectionary #21
Mt 3:13- 17
Lk 3:21-22
Mk 1:9/11

Situating the Homily

Last time we heard about Jesus (Christmas/Epiphany), Jesus was a baby/infant/child. Today, Jesus is already grown up.

What do you think Jesus did as he grew up? How do you think he spent his time?

Developing the Main Points

Among other things, Jesus prayed. Gradually, Jesus came to know what God the Father wanted him to do: bring people together as brothers and sisters, as God's family.

Jesus left home, left his mother, to answer God's call.

Jesus' baptism: we celebrate how Jesus responded to God's call:

- to reach out to all people

- to proclaim the message of God's love

Jesus said, "I accept!" He said "Yes!" to God and to his mission.

God the Father is so excited and happy! He tells us: "Listen to Jesus!"

Through our baptism, we try to:

- listen to Jesus

- do as Jesus does

- see as Jesus sees

- love as Jesus loves

Conclusion

In what ways can we—do we—say "yes" to God?

God is thrilled with us, too, as we respond to his call to follow God's Word and listen to Jesus!

Related Liturgical Suggestions:

Use the option of the sprinkling rite at the beginning of the liturgy.

 **Christian Unity**

Focus Group   **Notes**

General

**Liturgical/Scriptural
References**

Chair of Unity Octave
  (January)
Lectionary Series: #811-815
Jn 17:20-26

Situating the Homily

Do you have any brothers and sisters? Name them!

Do you have any cousins? Name them!

Often we're related to people who do not share the same
last name (certain aunts and uncles, cousins).

Developing the Main Points

In God's family, our name is *Catholic* but we have some
brothers and sisters, cousins and other relatives:

- Lutherans
- Baptists
- Episcopalians
- Methodists
- Presbyterians

These "relatives" go to (*name several local churches of other denominations*).

Our family name is *Catholic.* Along with the Orthodox churches, we are the oldest and the largest Christian family (*possibly mention some other local Catholic churches*). We believe that we are the church that Jesus himself started when he was on earth. That does not automatically make us superior; actually, it imposes more challenges.

Sometimes, like brothers and sisters and other relatives, we have "family feuds"; we fight with each other. This is not good; it is not what Jesus intended.

Conclusion

Being Catholic is a special privilege and a special responsibility to share God's message with all his people.

At the same time, we need to respect, to listen, to work with the other members of our Christian family, who are our relatives and cousins!

Related Liturgical Suggestions

Place pictures of local churches—especially of other Christian denominations—at the entrance or gathering space.

 **Christmas**

Focus Group

General

Liturgical/Scriptural References

December 25 and its Vigil
Lectionary #13
Lk 2:1-14

Notes

A small, gaily wrapped gift may serve as a prop. As the homily progresses, the preacher may throw it around, step on it, etc., as indicated in the outline.

Situating the Homily

Season of gifts: We spend much time and much money on choosing the right gift.

- What does the person need?
- What does the person like?
- What can he/she use?

We look long and hard for the right gift, the perfect gift, wrap it carefully, and look forward to giving it to the person.

Developing the Main Points

How would you feel if the person

- didn't appreciate it?
- just threw it in the closet?
- destroyed it?
- didn't even open it?

God gives us the gift of peace at Christmas. Angels tell us "Peace to God's people on earth."

He knows we need it. He knows we want it. He knows we can use it.

So many times, though, we don't want it, we don't appreciate it, and we don't use it.

Should we just throw it away? Should we just rip it up? (*Destroy the gift-wrapped box.*)

How can we use God's gift of peace? How can we unwrap God's gift of peace?

Conclusion

God gives us what we really need, what we really want, what we can really use. God gives us peace, gives us Jesus.

Use it! Make peace! Be at peace! This Christmas and always!

Related Liturgical Suggestions

Include a prayer in the intercessions for all the war-torn countries in the world. Perhaps have the children name the ones they know of, especially those countries where children are suffering.

Church As People

Focus Group

Notes

Intermediate Grades

Liturgical/Scriptural References

Mk 3:1-6
Lk 6:6-11

Situating the Homily

A church is a special building. Why? It is the house of God.

But where else does God live? In us!

Developing the Main Points

How do we respect this church building?

- Be being quiet
- By genuflecting/kneeling
- By making the sign of the cross
- By not speaking to those around us, even if we know them

Jesus respected his places of worship, but tells us the real dwelling place of God on this earth is *people.*

It is you. It is me. It is us—because Jesus dwells in us.

He says: My church is made out of people.

We are the carriers of God in this world! We are the
temples of the Holy Spirit! We bear the name of Jesus
Christ!

That is why it is so serious

- when people fight
- when people push and shove
- when people get other people in trouble
- when people don't talk to each other

Conclusion

We are the temples of God!

Related Liturgical Suggestions

Perhaps the sign of peace could be utilized at the end of
the homily as a sign of respect and reverence for one
another.

Closing Mass:
Religious Education Program

Focus Group

General

Liturgical/Scriptural References

Parable of the Sower
  (Mk 4:1-9)
Parable of the Fig Tree
  (Lk 13:6-9)

Notes

You will need a flower pot, potting soil, seeds/bulbs, and a watering can for this homily.

Situating the Homily

If we wanted this seed/bulb to grow, what would we have to do?

- Plant it.
- Water it.
- Give it sunshine.

What would happen if we forgot to water it? Of course, it won't grow.

All living things need water (*water flower pot*) to live.

Developing the Main Points

God gives life and love to us as seeds. The waters of baptism first awaken God's life within us, God's love for us.

That life and love continue to thrive and grow throughout our lives.

Jesus often spoke about growth (refer to the Gospel episode/parable).

Sacraments nourish us. Prayer nurtures us. Our Christian life is enriched in this process.

Every religion class is an opportunity to grow in God's life and love.

Conclusion

Today we celebrate another year of growth, a growth that began with our baptism.

This is reason to rejoice!

Keep growing!

Related Liturgical Suggestions

Use the option of the sprinkling rite at the beginning of the liturgy.

Discipleship: Imitation of Jesus

Focus Group

General

Notes

Liturgical/Scriptural References

St. Barnabas (June 11)
Lectionary #580
Acts 11:21-26, 13:1-3
Lk 8:19-21
Phil 4:8-9

Situating the Homily

In the game "Simon Says," who wins? (*the one who does everything and only the things that "Simon Says"*)

This is similar to how we live as Christians: we try to do everything and only the things that "Jesus Says."

Developing the Main Points

"Jesus says"

- Love one another.

- Pray all the time.

- Take care of yourself properly.

Today we hear how Saul and Barnabas were sent to share the Good News of Jesus with others.

Jesus says that we too are sent to share the Good News of Jesus with others; that is what we have to do.

Conclusion

If we do everything that "Jesus Says," then we will all be winners with Jesus!

Related Liturgical Suggestions

Conclude the Gospel by saying, "The Good News of the Lord."

Easter: Paschal Candle

Focus Group   **Notes**

Primary/Intermediate Grades

**Liturgical/Scriptural
References**

Lectionary #43
Jn 20:1-9

Situating the Homily

One of the hardest things in the world is keeping a
secret! You know about something that nobody else does
(or only one to two people do), such as:

- a surprise party
- who's dating who
- a Christmas present for someone!

You're bursting! You're dying to tell someone, tell the
news, share the surprise.

Developing the Main Points

The apostles knew about the resurrection of Jesus. They
couldn't keep it a secret. They shared it with everyone
and thus started the church.

The secret is still being shared with us today—two
thousand years later. One way we share the secret in our
church is to light the Easter paschal candle, which

- reminds us of the secret

- tells us Jesus is the light of the world
- tells us Jesus is alive and still with us

The secret of the resurrection is a secret for us to share!

How can we share the secret?

- by the way we live
- by the way we love
- by the way we act
- by the way we treat others

Conclusion

Don't keep it a secret. Spread it around!

Related Liturgical Suggestions

Carry the paschal candle in the opening procession, and place it in its place of honor in the sanctuary. Suggest to the children they light a paschal candle at home.

Use the option of the sprinkling rite at the beginning of the liturgy.

Epiphany 1

Focus Group

Intermediate Grades

Liturgical/Scriptural References

Lectionary #20

Mt 2:1-12

Notes

Have samples of the three gifts of the astrologers as props: (church) incense; balsamic vinegar for myrrh; and an ornamented box of "gold" jewelry and doubloons, if possible. Let the children see/ touch/smell the gifts during the homily. (Gold-wrapped chocolate coins might be effective as well.)

Situating the Homily

Today we recall some astrologers (sometimes referred to as "three wise men" or "three kings" in Christmas carols) who were determined to follow the star, for they knew it would lead them to Jesus. They came to find the child Jesus because he was important to them. Jesus is:

- the savior of the world
- God's son
- our brother

Developing the Main Points

It is customary to present important people with gifts. The gifts listed in the Gospel are expensive, exotic:

- *Gold*: valuable; riches, wealth, money. Jesus is valuable, rich in kindness and mercy. Gold represents his kingship all over the world.

- *Frankincense*: This is the same as incense (air-freshener); burning it makes a pleasing odor. The astrologer brought incense because he saw in Jesus the way to please God.

- *Myrrh*: bitter. The astrologer knew that Jesus, like all of us, would run into troubles and difficulties in everyday living. He also knew that he would need Jesus' help in time of trouble.

We bring the same gifts to Jesus today (in our Mass).

- He is our savior.

- We want to please him by imitating him.

- We know he is valuable and important.

- We need his help in the difficulties we face in living as Christians.

Conclusion

The astrologers brought gold, frankincense, and myrrh.

What gifts can we bring him? What kind of gifts do you think Jesus would enjoy/cherish the most?

On the other hand, Jesus is the great gift-giver himself: He gives eternal life, a rich life, a life of love.

Related Liturgical Suggestions

The use of incense in the opening procession and during the liturgy is most appropriate, as is its use throughout the entire Christmas season.

Use traditional Christmas carols in the liturgy, such as "We Three Kings" and "As With Gladness Men of Old." A number of other familiar carols contain references to the wise men in certain verses (e.g., "The First Noel," "What Child Is This?", and "O Holy Night.").

Epiphany 2

**Liturgical/Scriptural
References**

Lectionary #20
Mt 2:1-12

Situating the Homily

Did you ever go on a trip? What did you have to do to
get ready?

* make careful preparations

* get a map

* get directions

* make reservations

The most important thing we need to get ready for a trip
is a destination—we need someplace to go!

Developing the Main Points

Three wise astrologers followed a star even though they
had no idea of where it would take them. Somehow they
knew that it would lead them to Jesus, so they traveled
with open hearts and with open minds.

The star was a special sign from God so they traveled for
weeks, even months, just to find Jesus, God's gift of love.
And the star did indeed lead them to Jesus!

- They believed.
- They trusted.
- They followed.

Who are the stars in your life? Who are the people who

- taught you about Jesus?
- led you to Jesus?
- showed you God's love?

We are stars, too! We are sent by God to

- show the world how good and loving God is
- help others to find Jesus by the way we live, pray, and treat others.

Conclusion

We can be stars to one another; we can help people find Jesus just like the star helped/guided the astrologers to find Jesus. How can we be *brighter* stars?

We are stars because we show others the way to Jesus!

Related Liturgical Suggestions

As the children leave Mass, perhaps they could receive a "star" to wear throughout the day/week; an appropriate dismissal prayer could help reinforce the concept that they too are "stars" leading others to Jesus.

The use of incense in the opening procession and during the liturgy is most appropriate, as is its use throughout the entire Christmas season.

Use traditional Christmas carols in the liturgy, such as "We Three Kings" and "As With Gladness Men of Old." A number of other familiar carols contain references to the wise men in certain verses (e.g., "The First Noel," "What Child Is This?", and "O Holy Night.").

Eucharistic Gifts

Focus Group

Intermediate Grades

Liturgical/Scriptural References

Corpus Christi
  (Lectionary Series #168-70)
20th Sunday of the Year (B)
Votive Mass of the Holy Eucharist
  (Lectionary #904-909)
First Communion
Jn 6:51-58

Notes

Use the bread and wine that will be used for communion to illustrate.

Situating the Homily

Boys and girls, everyone I know loves to give—and get!—presents!

When we gather for Mass, we give gifts to God. What gifts do we give?

Developing the Main Points

From what you are telling me, it seems we give God gifts of love, praise, and thanks.

How do we show our love, praise, and thanks?

How do we give God these gifts at Mass?

What do we use?

- bread and wine

In giving bread and wine, we give ourselves with Jesus to God the Father. And you know what? God is delighted with our gifts!

He takes them, touches them, transforms them, and give them back to us!

The bread and wine become Jesus, and God gives Jesus to us in them (holy communion) so that we can continue to transform our lives and hearts and become more like Jesus.

Conclusion

We give God gifts, and he returns our gifts so we can share them, share our lives and love—share Jesus—with others!

Related Liturgical Suggestions

Use bread the children have baked for the liturgy. Be sure the cup is available to all at communion.

Evangelists/Evangelization

Focus Group

Primary/Intermediate Grades

Liturgical/Scriptural References

Saint Matthew (Sep 21):
Mt 9:9-13; Lect #643
Saint Mark (Apr 25):
Mk 16:15-20; Lect #555
Saint Luke (Oct 18): Lk 10:1-9;
Lect #661
Saint John (Dec 27): Jn 20:2-8;
Lect #697

Notes

A megaphone—easily made from a large sheet of construction paper—is a necessary prop for this homily.

Situating the Homily

What is this thing? (*Hold up megaphone.*)

What do you use it for? (*demonstrate*)

- make voice louder
- communicate more effectively
- help people understand you better
- help people hear you better (loud and clear)
- give directions
- rise above the noise

Developing the Main Points

Evangelists are friends of Jesus who are like megaphones:

- They tell us *loud and clear* about Jesus.

- They help us understand Jesus.

- They give directions on how to live like Jesus by their words, by their activities, by their faith, by the way they lives their lives.

We too are evangelists. As Christians we are supposed to tell other people *loud and clear* about Jesus. In this way we are also evangelists!

Conclusion

How can we do that?

Related Liturgical Suggestions

Place a picture, icon, or statue of the evangelist at the entrance or in the gathering area.

First Holy Communion 1

Focus Group

Primary Grades

Liturgical/Scriptural References

Mass of Christian Initiation
Lectionary Series #752-756
Votive Mass of the Holy Eucharist
Lectionary Series #904-909

Notes

A can of spinach may serve as a simple prop.

Situating the Homily

Is everyone familiar with the cartoon character Popeye?

What does Popeye always eat?

What does spinach do for him?

It makes him strong!

That's what our mothers are always telling us!

Sometimes our mothers tell us carrots are good for our eyes, that fish are brain food, or that onions put hair on our chests.

Developing the Main Points

What our mothers are really trying to tell us is that the food we eat is important. Food affects our bodies, our health, our well-being. Certain foods that are really good for us are milk, fruit, and vegetables. We need a healthy variety!

Foods that are not so good are too much candy, sugar, soda, and other junk food.

One very special food that our bodies, our lives, and our hearts need is Jesus, whom we receive in holy communion.

Actually, Jesus is the most important thing we need. Every time we receive holy communion, the bread and wine, it nourishes our hearts and feeds our souls so that we can become more loving people, more like Jesus.

The more we receive holy communion, the easier it is to love God, neighbor, and self.

Conclusion

Holy communion *makes a difference!*

Holy communion is really good for us. We need to receive Jesus often. We need it; the world needs it; we all need more Jesus.

Related Liturgical Suggestions

Use home-baked bread for communion. Be sure the communion cup is available to all at communion time.

First Holy Communion 2

Focus Group

Primary Grades

Liturgical/Scriptural References

Mass of Christian Initiation
Lectionary Series #752-756
Votive Mass of the Holy Eucharist
Lectionary Series #904-909

Notes

An empty McDonald's Happy Meal box may serve as a simple prop.

Situating the Homily

How many of you have ever been to McDonald's?

How many of you have ever had a Happy Meal?

What's in a Happy Meal?

- various food items
- a special prize, a special gift

Developing the Main Points

A McDonald's Happy Meal is not the only meal that is a "happy meal."

- Every time we go to church...
- Every time we go to Mass...

...we participate in a "happy meal."

Why do you think that is so?

At Mass, we hear about God and his love for us. We hear about Jesus and how we should live, how we should love.

- Sing songs.
- Say prayers with our families and friends.
- Do all the things that make us happy to be together.

And at Mass we receive a special gift as well. What do you think it is? Who is it?

The gift is Jesus himself in holy communion, in the bread and wine.

Today, as always, we celebrate a happy meal, one of the happiest meals we can have because for the first time you boys and girls will receive Jesus in holy communion.

Conclusion

I am very proud of you, boys and girls, and I hope that you will share in many happy meals and receive Jesus into your hearts. He really is a special gift!

Related Liturgical Suggestions

Use home-baked bread for communion. Be sure the communion cup is available to all at communion time.

First Reconciliation

Focus Group   Notes

Primary Grades

**Liturgical/Scriptural
References**

Parable of the Prodigal Son
Lk 15:11-32

Situating the Homily

Sometimes, we are like the boy in the story.

- We run away from God.

- We run away from other people.

- We turn our backs on them and say, "No! These
  are *my* toys! I want it *my* way. It's *my* turn!"

- We turn selfish: Me! Me! Me! Gimme! Mine! Me!

Developing the Main Points

When we behave like this, God our Father feels sad. Our
parents/families feel sad. Our friends feel sad. They still
love us, but we leave them behind; we don't want to be
bothered.

The time comes to say "I'm sorry."

The time comes to go back home.

The time comes to go back to loving them.

Surprise! They are waiting for us with open arms. Confession gives us a chance to do just that, a chance to start all over again.

Conclusion

When it is time to come home, confession brings us back together, again and again: you, me, Jesus!

Related Liturgical Suggestions

As a way of emphasizing the Lord's Prayer—a prayer of reconciliation—invite everyone to pray it with their hands joined or with their arms extended and palms upturned.

Grandparents Celebration

Focus Group

Intermediate Grades

Notes

**Liturgical/Scriptural
References**

Sir 44:1, 10-15
Mt 13:16-17
Lk 2:22-40

Situating the Homily

Boys and girls, how would you define the word "grand"?

In general, what does it mean to say that something is grand?

Boys and girls, what makes grandparents grand? (*Answers will vary; relate their comments to the previously elicited definitions, especially as they apply to grandparents.*)

Developing the Main Points

So many things make our grandparents grand, and for them we thank God.

For they are very special people to us. Their love for us and our love for them makes them truly grand—and makes us truly their *grand*children!

Conclusion

Actually, in God's eyes, all people are grand. How can we show people that we recognize how grand they are?

Related Liturgical Suggestions

Include the sign of peace at the conclusion of the homily.

Greatest Commandment

Focus Group   **Notes**

Junior High Students

Liturgical/Scriptural References

Friday/3rd Week of Lent
31st Sunday of the Year (B)
Mk 12:28-34

Situating the Homily

It seems to me that people were always asking Jesus questions. Can anyone remember some of the questions that people asked Jesus?

- "Who is my neighbor?"
- "How should we pray?"
- "What must I do to gain eternal life?"
- "Where do you live?"

Developing the Main Points

What was the scribe's question in today's Gospel? (*"What is the first of all the commandments?"*)

What was Jesus' answer?

- love of God
- love of neighbor
- love of self

In today's Gospel, we have the *only* time when someone agrees with Jesus, even compliments him on his answer: "Excellent, Teacher!" Usually people argued, disagreed, or debated with Jesus.

But now I have a question for you.

What do *you* think of Jesus' answer? Would you give Jesus an A+ or 100%? Was it a good answer? Was it the "right" answer? Was it really "excellent"?

If we believe that Jesus is right/correct/true, what does that mean we should do?

And how should we do it?

Conclusion

Jesus' answer *is* the right answer. If you have the questions, Jesus has the answers.

Jesus is the answer!

Related Liturgical Suggestions

Pray Eucharistic Prayer I, using the names of all the saints listed there as examples of people who knew Jesus' love was the answer.

Halloween (Vigil: All Saints)

Focus Group   Notes

Primary/Intermediate Grades

Liturgical/Scriptural References

Vigil of All Saints
Lectionary #667
Mt 5:1-12

Situating the Homily

On Halloween, we wear different kinds of costumes:

- movie stars
- cartoon characters
- saints
- public figures

We dress up like them. We think it's neat. Maybe we act like them, too.

- Monsters/ghosts scare people.
- Hard guys act tough.
- Movie stars act glamorous.

Maybe we talk like them, too; maybe we try to trick people. Basically, on Halloween, we try to be someone else.

Developing the Main Points

All Saints Day and Halloween remind us to be like somebody else—to be like Jesus. Maybe we don't dress up like Jesus, but we can act like him. Did Jesus:

- scare people?
- hurt people?
- trick people?

No. To act like Jesus means to:

- love God
- love neighbor
- take care of yourself

We don't have to dress up like Jesus to be like Jesus. We can just be ourselves.

We can have the "attitudes of the Beatitudes":

- We can be patient.
- We can be peacemakers.
- We can be more like God's children.
- We can remain strong in our faith in Jesus in the face of difficulties.

Conclusion

Let's try hard to be like Jesus, okay? How can we do that, starting tonight?

Related Liturgical Suggestions

Decorate the church with pumpkins carved with crosses of various shapes and designs (e.g., Jerusalem cross, Celtic cross, traditional cross, etc.). Doing so will help set an atmosphere in keeping with All Saints.

 **Initiation**

Focus Group

General

Liturgical/Scriptural References

Lectionary Series #752-756

Notes

For use in the Rite of Christian Initiation of Children.

Situating the Homily

Sometimes it's good and right to say "no." When is it a good idea to say "no"? (*e.g., to strangers, to drugs, etc.*)

Sometimes it's good and right to say "yes!"

What does it mean to say "yes" to someone?

Developing the Main Points

Today we celebrate because you are saying "yes" to God in a very special and permanent way.

You say "yes" to God the Father/Creator when you

- accept God's love
- join God's family, the church
- live in love with others
- listen to God's Word and take it to heart

By saying "yes" to God the Son/Redeemer, you

- accept the name "Christian"
- imitate Jesus' example

- grow in knowledge of God and his Message
- pattern your life after Jesus

By saying "yes" to God the Holy Spirit/Sanctifier, you

- are empowered to live as a Christian
- desire to serve others
- praise God for God's goodness to you
- use your talents and gifts for the good of God's people and the world

Conclusion

Today you are saying a great big "yes" to a close relationship with God for the rest of your life!

Keep on saying "yes" to God!

Related Liturgical Suggestions

Use the option of the sprinkling rite at the beginning of the liturgy.

Life Is Unfair

Focus Group

Intermediate Groups

Liturgical/Scriptural References

Lk 23:35-43

Notes

Provide a gift/treat for only three or four of the children to illustrate injustice.

Situating the Homily

I have a treat for you today! We can enjoy it together! (*Distribute treats to a select few.*)

Isn't this great? No?

Why? How do you feel about not getting a treat? Is it fair?

(*Ask those who did not receive a treat:*) How do you feel about getting a treat when others did not get one? Is it fair?

Should anything be done about this? If so, what?

Developing the Main Points

We often believe that we have been treated unfairly:

- left out of a group
- yelled at
- criticized harshly
- not listened to
- stolen from

- called names
- laughed at

Jesus was also treated unfairly, so he understands how we feel when we are not treated right.

Because we know what it's like, too, we can feel and be concerned for others when they are not treated fairly.

Jesus prayed for those who nailed him to the cross and made fun of him. "Father, forgive them...."

Conclusion

Let's try to be like Jesus when people don't treat us right.

Let's not respond in anger or in hatred.

We can reach out to others when they are being hurt. How can we do this?

Let's try to treat others fairly at all times (positive thrust)!

Related Liturgical Suggestions

Be sure not to use any communion from the tabernacle in order to avoid giving newly consecrated bread to only a select few. Be sure everyone has the opportunity to share from the cup.

Listening to God's Word

Focus Group

Primary Grades

Notes

Liturgical/Scriptural References

Thursday/Second Week of Lent
Lectionary #234
26th Sunday of the Year (C)
Lectionary #139
Lk 16:19- 31

Situating the Homily

What are some things you might like to hear?

- "No school today!"

- "Let's go to McDonald's."

- the bell at the end of the school day

What are some things you might not like to hear?

- "Wait till we get home."

- "You're in for it now."

- "I'm telling...."

- alarm clock in the morning

Developing the Main Points

What are some of your favorite words?

As Christians, we hear great things, the Good News, God our Father/Mother speaking to us in a special way in the Bible.

We hear the prophets.

We listen to the evangelists.

We pay attention to the sacred authors.

We *listen* to Jesus!

Let's just take a moment to focus on *listening*.

Be very quiet.

Make yourself comfortable. Close your eyes.

Listen to what your hear...in silence.

God works especially well in our lives when we're quiet, when we make the effort to listen, when we open our minds/hearts/lives to God in silence.

Conclusion

It's the best way to hear one of our favorite sounds: the Word of God speaking to our hearts in receptive silence.

It's a message, a sound, a word of love!

Related Liturgical Suggestions

After the homily, allow for an extended silence.

Mary, Mother of Jesus

Focus Group

Primary/Intermediate Grades

Liturgical/Scriptural References

Annunciation: March 25
Lectionary #545
Lk 1:26-38
Marian Celebrations

Situating the Homily

In today's Gospel, Mary says "yes" to God.

What would have happened if Mary had said "no"?

* no Jesus

* no Christmas

But she said "yes!" Thank you, Mary!

All her life, Mary said "yes" to God:

* Mary helped Jesus with his homework.

* Mary wiped Jesus' running nose.

* Mary made chocolate chip cookies for Jesus and Joseph.

* Mary washed Jesus' clothes.

* Mary worried about Jesus, prayed for him, and laughed with him.

Developing the Main Points

Jesus grew up and went away to do God's work.

Mary supported, encouraged, and prayed for him. Then she experienced sad times.

Jesus had some hard times. He:

- suffered.

- was rejected.

- was mocked.

When Jesus was on the cross, Mary was there.

Jesus always thought of others, even on the cross. He might have said to Mary, "Mom, I feel so sorry for you—so alone, so afraid. I didn't want you to see this, Mom. You are so lonely, so lost, so upset." Jesus gave her all the children of the world to care for:

- to pray for

- to guide

She became our mother to help us become better friends of her son, Jesus.

Conclusion

We honor Mary as our mother, our helper, our queen. Stay close to Mary, our heavenly mother; she will help us draw closer to Jesus!

Related Liturgical Suggestions

Place an icon, picture, or statue of Mary at the entrance or in the gathering space.

Mary: Visitation of Elizabeth

Focus Group   Notes

Intermediate Grades

Liturgical/Scriptural
References

Visitation (May 31)
Lk 1:39-56
Lectionary #572

Situating the Homily

Have you ever visited anyone? Who? When? Where? Why?

What's it like to visit someone—a friend, perhaps, or a family member (grandparents)?

Developing the Main Points

Why did Mary visit Elizabeth?

Instant Replay: What happened to Mary just before she went to visit Elizabeth? (*Annunciation*)

Angel Gabriel told her: "Hail, Mary! You are full of God's life! The Lord is with you!"

God was with Mary in a very deep, very profound way.

Mary was touched by God to be the Mother of Jesus, God's own Son.

When she realized that God had touched her in a new and powerful way, her first impulse was to help those in need. So off she went to help Elizabeth.

When we let God touch us, wonderful things can happen. We respond to the needs of people around us.

Conclusion

How can we respond to the needs of those around us?

- Visit people.

- Spend time with people.

- Listen to people.

Let God touch *you* and see what happens!

Related Liturgical Suggestions:

Place an icon, picture, or statue of Mary at the entrance or in the gathering space.

Mission Awareness

Focus Group

General

Liturgical/Scriptural References

Lectionary Series #816-820
Pastoral celebrations of Holy
  Childhood, World Mission
  Sunday, general mission
  appeals

Notes

Situating the Homily

S-T-R-E-T-C-H!

Have you ever stretched?

- Tired? Stretch!
- Stiff? Stretch!

Stretching helps us

- feel better
- stay in shape
- get ready for action

Developing the Main Points

Athletes stretch in order to:

- warm up for exercise

- prepare themselves to do well

- reach a little further

- move a little quicker

- perform a little better

Through your support of our missionaries, you help missionaries throughout the world to "stretch" a little more:

- help them reach out a little further with an extra Band-Aid

- help them hand out another slice of bread to a hungry child

- help them travel to distant villages to spread the Good News and touch people with Jesus!

Your help makes it possible for missionaries to stretch a little more, reach a little further, do more good, help more people. Missionaries

- heal

- teach

- help others believe

They stretch your prayers/money/concern/assistance in order to help people whose lives are broken by war, poverty, disease, ignorance.

Conclusion

Help them stretch! Keep stretching! Support our missionaries!

Related Liturgical Suggestions

Use the intercessions and the blessing from the "Order for the Blessing of Missionaries" from the *Book of Blessings*.

 **Missionaries**

Focus Group　　　　　　　　**Notes**

General

Liturgical/Scriptural References

Ascension Thursday
  (Mk 16:15-20)
Lectionary #59
Conversion of St. Paul
  (January 25)
Lectionary #519
Any Feast/Memorial of a
  missionary (e.g., St. Francis
  Xavier, December 3)

Situating the Homily

What are missionaries? What do they do?
Who would like to be a missionary when you get older?

Developing the Main Points

You don't have to wait until you're older to be a
missionary. You already are!

The word "missionary" means "one who is sent." God
sends us into our...

- homes

- classrooms

- neighborhoods

...to do just what you told me a few moments ago. (*Refer to their answers of a moment ago, and emphasize the pertinent responses.*)

For whom can we do these things here and now, in our area, in our little corner of God's kingdom?

Conclusion

You are missionaries already. I hope you take the job seriously because I know you'll do—are already doing—a great job!

Related Liturgical Suggestions

Use the intercessions and the blessing from the "Order for the Blessing of Missionaries" from the *Book of Blessings*.

Papacy: Chair of Peter

Focus Group

Primary Grades

Liturgical/Scriptural References

February 22
Lectionary #535
1 Pt 5:1-4
Mt 16:13-19

Notes

Have a collection of keys—your own!—available for display.

Situating the Homily

Does anyone have any keys with you? If you have any, hold them up. Wow, so many keys!

I have a number of keys, too.

- This one—house keys
- That one—church keys
- This one—car keys

Developing the Main Points

What do we need keys for? What do they do?

- open or lock doors
- start or stop engines

In today's Gospel, Jesus gives Peter "the keys of the kingdom."

Our pope is successor to Peter. He has a special job to do. His job is the same as Peter's job was. The pope helps us stay open to:

- God's will
- God's Word (Jesus)
- God's Spirit
- each other

The pope also helps close off sin, division, barriers. He helps keep us united.

What is our pope's name? (*Or refer to the current pope by name wherever appropriate.*)

Conclusion

Today, pray for the pope that he does his job well!

Related Liturgical Suggestions

Be sure to include a prayer for the pope in the intercessions.

Peacemakers

Focus Group

Notes

Primary Grades

Liturgical/Scriptural References

Mt 5:1-12
Rom 12:9-21
Eph 5:18b-21
Col 3:5-11

Situating the Homily

What is a peacemaker? How do you "make" peace?

- with our hearts
- with our minds
- with our hands

Developing the Main Points

Saint Paul tells us how not to make peace:

- say bad things about each other
- lose your temper
- hold grudges
- raise your voice to anyone
- call each other names

These are ways to make trouble!

Instead, Paul tells us to

- speak the truth
- do good for others
- be friendly with everyone
- be kind
- forgive each other readily

That's how we make peace!

Conclusion

What are the advantages of "making peace"?

Related Liturgical Suggestions

Include the sign of peace after the homily as an indication of how we can use our hands to make peace.

Penitential Reflection

Focus Group

Junior High Students

Liturgical/Scriptural References

Ez 36:26-28

Jer 31:31-34

Notes

As a simple aid in this reflection, hand out small rocks (possibly marble chips, available at any nursery) to each student. For added effect, put the rocks in a freezer overnight. The students hold on to the rocks, feeling them, rolling them around in their hands, during this reflection.

Situating the Homily

We all carry rocks

- in our hearts

- in our minds

- in our lives

There are rocks of resentment: "She was picked; I wasn't."

There are rocks of hurt: "My parents split up; why did this happen to my family?"

There are rocks of loss: "The team didn't win."

And there are rocks of guilt: "If anyone ever knew...."

Developing the Main Points

Instead of carrying these rocks around, give them to the Lord:

- Throw them out.

- Cast them away.

- Get rid of them!

Prayer is a way of removing the rocks of bitterness, hurt, resentment, anger, trouble at home and in relationships.

You might pray,

> "Jesus, take this rock from me.
> I offer you my pain, my hurt, my sadness,
>   and my fear.
> Please, do something with it.
> Transform it for me.
> Let me get on with my life."

Did you ever get a stone in your shoe? Isn't it surprising how a little pebble can make us so uncomfortable, cause chronic pain, trip us up, and demand so much of our attention?

Like the stone in your shoe, sin can take up a lot of your time and energy and attention. Sin "trips us up" and gets in the way of our being the Christians we would like to be—and can be.

We all have rocks in our hearts (and sometimes we have rocks in our heads, too!). We all carry rocks in our lives.

Get rid of them!

Focus on the rock in your hand. Let it symbolize the sin that preoccupies you the most, that troubles you the most. Let it bear your pain, your guilt, your failures.

(After a brief period of reflective silence, drop/bury your rock in either:

- *a bowl of baptismal water [that gift of God
  that washes away all our sins and graces us
  with freedom]*

or

- *a wastebasket located at the foot of a crucifix
  ["Leave your sins at the feet of the Lord."]*

*If you are offering individual sacramental confession,
continue with the following:)*

Confession/Reconciliation

Even pebbles can eventually fill up a bucket, making it
heavy. In the same way, sinful actions and attitudes can
fill up our hearts, making them cold, stony, and hard.

Confession is way of getting rid of the rocks of sin in
your life; reconciliation is an opportunity to regain a
warm, loving heart.

Why carry the burden/rock of your sins?

*(After confession, invite the students to repeat your
actions as above:)*

Take your rock and drop (bury) it in this bowl of
baptismal water (wastebasket by crucifix).

Conclusion

As Christians, after confessing/admitting our sins, we feel
lighter, freer. Always turn to the Lord for help; get rid of
the "rocks"of sin in your lives!

Related Liturgical Suggestions

As a way of emphasizing the Lord's Prayer—a prayer of
reconciliation and receptivity—invite everyone to pray it
with their arms extended and palms upturned, for their
hands are no longer burdened with their "rocks."

Pentecost 1

Focus Group

Primary Grades

Liturgical/Scriptural References

Lectionary Series #63-64

Notes

Use a pinwheel as a prop for this homily.

Situating the Homily

(*Hold up pinwheel.*) How does this thing work? It just lays here; it doesn't do anything!

What can we do to make it "come alive"?

Developing the Main Points

We need wind, breath, motion, or a breeze to make it come to life!

The Holy Spirit is usually described as wind, breath, motion. God's Spirit makes us come alive as Christians. The more the Spirit is active in our lives, the more alive we are!

How would we then be different? (*Responses will vary.*)

Conclusion

We need the "breath" of the Holy Spirit to keep us alive, keep us moving, keep us active as Christians!

Related Liturgical Suggestions

Use the option of the sprinkling rite at the beginning of Mass to link Pentecost with Easter.

Pentecost 2

Focus Group

Primary Grades

Liturgical/Scriptural References

Lectionary Series #63-64

Notes

For this homily, prepare a large red balloon (deflated). On one side, draw a design (either a cross or Chi-Rho). Use this empty balloon as a prop during the homily as indicated.

Situating the Homily

Before Jesus called them, the apostles were slow, good for nothing, bland, flat, common ordinary folk. (*Show blank side of balloon.*)

Then Jesus called them, and the apostles became different. (*Show design side.*)

- They saw him working.
- They heard his preaching.
- They felt his loving.

Developing the Main Points

Still, Jesus' ways didn't always make sense to the apostles.

They just didn't "get it"; they didn't understand. But then, at Pentecost, the Spirit came and filled them up. (*Blow up balloon.*)

Then they understood! Everything clicked! The Spirit started to make a difference in their lives! (*Tie balloon.*)

Now they were free to spread Jesus' peace and love and joy to everyone. (*Toss balloon up and over the children's heads.*)

That's what the Spirit does for us:

- frees us

- helps us to understand

- fills us up

- gives us direction and responsibility

- commissions us

Conclusion

We have all already received the Spirit in baptism. So let the Spirit fill your life in all directions.

Related Liturgical Suggestions

Use the option of the sprinkling rite at the beginning of Mass to link Pentecost with Easter.

Give out red balloons (helium-filled) as Mass concludes. Tie the string around the children's wrists as they leave so none of the balloons end up on the ceiling of the church.

Pentecost 3

Focus Group

Intermediate Grades

Liturgical/Scriptural References

Lectionary Series #63-64

Notes

Have a small toy—preferably a robot or other small item—that needs batteries to operate. Keep batteries separate, to be inserted during the homily.

Situating the Homily

Many toys need batteries to operate; however, when we buy many battery-operated toys, the package usually tells us, "Batteries not included!"

Battery-operated toys are fun, but they are useless unless the proper batteries are inserted. Without batteries, some toys are just lifeless hunks of metal or plastic.

Developing the Main Points

(Insert batteries into toy and push "start" button to activate.)

See what a difference batteries make!

All of us, as Christians, need the Holy Spirit to...

- activate us.
- animate us.
- stimulate us.

The Spirit is the source of our power as Christians.

- The Spirit gives us strength and power.

- The Spirit breathes life into our faith.

We first received the Spirit at baptism, and we celebrate the Spirit in a special way today.

Two of the principal effects of the Spirit's power and presence in us are:

- The Spirit assists us to build up community.
- The Spirit enables us to relate well to one another.

We are "empowered" by the Holy Spirit just like this toy is "empowered" by the batteries.

Thus we are able to:

- heal hurts
- listen well
- challenge each other to grow

Conclusion

The Holy Spirit

- makes us strong
- gives us courage
- drives away fear
- empowers us
- keeps up going, and going, and going!

Related Liturgical Suggestions

Use the option of the sprinkling rite at the beginning of Mass to link Pentecost with Easter.

 **Pentecost 4**

Focus Group   **Notes**

Intermediate/Junior High

**Liturgical/Scriptural
References**

Lectionary Series #63-64

Situating the Homily

This is a season of promise, the promise of the coming of the Holy Spirit.

On Pentecost, the Holy Spirit descends into the church. The Spirit is a gift of the Father to all of us!

Developing the Main Points

We carry the Holy Spirit within us!

We first received the Spirit at baptism and celebrate that fact today in a special way.

But too often we keep the Spirit locked up; we don't allow the Spirit to operate, to influence us with the Spirit's

- vision
- power
- energy

Instead, we let...

- fear

- jealousy

- pettiness

...operate too often in our lives.

We mock/hassle/pick on/ignore others.

We need to pray to cooperate with the Holy Spirit, who will lead us to a better, happier life.

(Possibly refer to the gifts and fruits of the Holy Spirit.)

Conclusion

Don't keep the Holy Spirit locked up!

- Let the Holy Spirit move.

- Let the Holy Spirit help.

- Let the Holy Spirit guide you.

You hold the key!

Related Liturgical Suggestions

Use the option of the sprinkling rite at the beginning of Mass to link Pentecost with Easter.

Prayer and Christian Living

Focus Group

Junior High Students

Liturgical/Scriptural References

5th Sunday (B)
Wednesday of the First Week
  (Years I and II)
Wednesday of the 22nd Week
  (Years I and II)
Mk 1:35-39
Lk 4:42-44

Notes

Construct a simple traffic light out of a clean milk carton, and use it during the homily as a simple prop.

Situating the Homily

What do the colors on a traffic light mean?

- Red = Stop!
- Yellow = Caution!
- Green = Go!

These colors make a lot of sense for safety's sake.

Developing the Main Points

The colors of a traffic light remind me of a pattern in Jesus' life that is a good idea for us in our Christian lives today.

Jesus would often *stop*, making time for prayer, especially when confronted by questions, challenges, problems, difficulties (e.g., the temptations in the desert). Jesus took these concerns to prayer.

He used *caution*.

- He prayed over these concerns.

- He explored options.

- He listened to others as he did God his Father.

- He took the time for prayer and reflection.

Then, he would *go*!

Jesus reached decisions and acted on them. His actions helped himself and others

- to be more faithful

- to be more determined to do God's will (e.g., agony in the garden)

Jesus' actions were usually expressed in a burst of teaching and healing activity.

Conclusion

Stop. Look and listen. Do. This is a very necessary process for us as Christians.

We need the Spirit's guidance to find a balance of prayer/reflection and action.

Many difficult issues face us as Christians. Many issues face us as human beings.

Do what Jesus did: Take time to stop, look/listen/pray, then go ahead!

Related Liturgical Suggestions

Allow for extended silences after each of the readings and the homily in order to "listen."

 **St. Blaise**

Focus Group　　　　**Notes**

General

**Liturgical/Scriptural
References**

February 3
Mass or prayer service
Lectionary #525
Options #713-718 or #719-724
Any healing episode from the
　Gospels

Situating the Homily

Today we remember St. Blaise, who was

- a bishop in Asia Minor
- shrouded in legend

The most familiar story related about him is one in which he cures a boy who had a fish bone lodged in his throat and who was choking to death.

Developing the Main Points

We remember St. Blaise as a friend of those who are sick, especially with sicknesses and diseases of the throat (sore throats, strep throat, laryngitis, coughs, cancer of the throat, etc.).

We ask him to pray with us and for us for good health (both mind and body), especially the good health of our throats.

We believe that our God is a God of healing. We believe God wants us to be well/healthy/safe/holy. God's Son, Jesus, spent much of his time healing.

We thank God especially today for the gift of good health and the gift of our breath. Our celebration today reminds us not to take good health for granted nor abuse our health.

How can we take better care of our health, this gift God has given us? (*Take our vitamins, dress properly to stay warm, etc.*)

Conclusion

As I bless your throats today, ask St. Blaise to help us take care of our health and to help us appreciate the gift of good health.

That's what God wishes for us—that we be

- happy
- holy ("whole")
- healthy

Related Liturgical Suggestions

Distribute peppermint candies at the end of the Mass or prayer service. As the children suck on the candy, tell them to breathe through their mouths and feel the "tingly" sensation; use this activity as an opportunity to reflect on the gift of our breath, our health, our very life!

St. Francis of Assisi

Focus Group   **Notes**

Intermediate/Junior High

**Liturgical/Scriptural
References**

October 4
Lectionary #651
cf. Mk 10:17-30

Situating the Homily

Today we celebrate a remarkable man: Francis of Assisi.
Francis is one of the most popular saints of all time.

After a rowdy adolescence and after months of
imprisonment (as a prisoner of war) and sickness, he
experienced a complete change of heart.

Developing the Main Points

Francis realized that he must take the Gospel to heart; he
realized that God is serious. So he began caring for the
sick and helping the poor. He even became poor himself.

What is poverty? What is it like to be poor? For Francis,
poverty meant

- total trust in God
- total dependence on God
- no possessions
- give everything to the poor

Francis constantly preached peace and God's love for all creation, and he found God in all creation. Everything, everyone reminded him of God:

- fire
- children
- birds
- animals
- life

He spoke of the sun, moon, wind, and earth as his brothers and sisters. He firmly believed that we are all part of God's family—and that made him genuinely happy, joyful.

Francis spent his life trying to help people see and experience the presence of God in their daily lives.

Conclusion

Is God present in our daily lives? How? Why? Where?

Francis reminds us to take notice of God in everyone and in everything!

Related Liturgical Suggestions:

Illustrate the "Canticle of the Sun" with students' artwork or slides.

Use one of various musical arrangements of "The Peace Prayer of St. Francis."

Develop the theme of peacemakers.

St. John the Baptist

Focus Group

Intermediate Grades

Notes

Liturgical/Scriptural References

Advent liturgies
Sundays of Advent: 2nd (ABC),
   3rd (BC)
Weekdays as appropriate

Situating the Homily

Today we run into (again) a rather odd person, John the Baptist (Baptizer)

Who is he? What do we know about him?

- Elizabeth and Zechariah were his parents.

- He was a cousin of Jesus.

- He was designated from conception to be a messenger of God.

- Mary visited Elizabeth when she was pregnant with John.

- John lived and preached in the desert.

- He ate locusts (grasshoppers) and wild honey.

- He wore animal skins.

Developing the Main Points

People came from all over to listen to him. Why? Why is John so important?

- His message was to turn away from sin and be baptized.

- His mission was to prepare the way for Jesus and God's salvation.

He spoke the truth. He kept insisting:

- Get ready for Jesus!

- Put aside sinful ways!

- Help other people!

- Pray!

- Be faithful!

- Love God completely!

- Keep an eye out for Jesus!

Conclusion

We always need to get ready for Jesus; we need to stay focused on Jesus and the Gospel.

How can we do that?

John the Baptist:

- Get ready.

- Get set for Jesus!

Related Liturgical Suggestions

Place a picture, icon, or statue of John the Baptist at the entrance or in the gathering space.

 **St. Joseph**

Focus Group

Intermediate Grades

Notes

Liturgical/Scriptural References

Feast of the Holy Family
  (March 19)
St. Joseph the Worker (May 1)

Situating the Homily

Notice the man in the background of this Gospel passage. Who is he?

Joseph took the role of Jesus' father on earth.

- He loved Jesus.

- He raised him.

- He protected him.

- He taught him how to work with wood (carpentry).

- Even more so, Joseph taught Jesus values—the things in life that are important.

What do you think are some of the values that Joseph shared with Jesus?

Really, Joseph taught Jesus about life and love not only by what he said but, more importantly, by what he did—in fact, there is no record of him *saying* anything in the Gospels!

Developing the Main Points

Joseph was a quiet, gentle man who

- loved very much
- worked very hard
- believed very deeply

Joseph did everything with

- a touch of gentleness
- a touch of humor
- a touch of God

He did nothing fancy or out of the ordinary, but he left a big impression on Jesus, who in turn left us a good example to follow.

Conclusion

What can we learn from Joseph? The same things Jesus apparently did!

Related Liturgical Suggestions

Provide the children with an adapted version of the "Order of the Blessing of St. Joseph's Table" from the *Book of Blessings* for use at home.

As you begin the homily, point out the statue or stained glass window of St. Joseph (if available) in your church.

 **St. Nicholas**

Focus Group   Notes

Primary/Intermediate Grades

Liturgical/Scriptural References

December 6

Lectionary #687 (#719-724)

Situating the Homily

Where does the legend of Santa Claus come from? Let me tell you a story about someone named Saint Nicholas.

Developing the Main Points

Long ago, the bishop of Myra was a very important man. He wore vestments such as a miter and carried a staff (crosier). He helped people to be close to Jesus. He loved people like Jesus did. He was generous and kind.

In his town there was a poor family named Orlando. Mr. Orlando's three daughters could not get married because they were so poor. They had a bleak future; anything could happen to them.

One night, St. Nicholas heard the girls crying at home. He threw some money through their window to help.

He enjoyed sneaking around at night to the homes of poor people, leaving them food, clothing, some money. He was a real gift-giver! Everybody loved Nicholas. In time, people came to remember him by giving gifts themselves.

The story of St. Nicholas traveled to Holland, where the people really like this story. In their language, when they said "Saint Nicholas" they said "Sinter Klaas." They would imagine St. Nicholas riding a big white horse through the neighborhood with his helper, Peter. Dutch children remember St. Nicholas by hanging stockings on their bedroom doors or putting shoes outside their rooms to receive gifts from St. Nicholas if they're good! Sometimes they left hay for the horse. St. Nicholas Day became a day for giving gifts.

When some of these Dutch people came to America, they brought the custom with them, but in English, "Sinter Klaas" became "Santa Claus." St. Nicholas' bishop's clothes became a red suit; his funny hat became a snow cap; his staff became a candy cane.

As time went on, St. Nicholas' helper, Peter, became Santa Claus' elves; his vehicle became a sleigh and reindeer. Just like St. Nicholas, Santa Claus leaves gifts in our Christmas stockings. Instead of leaving hay for a horse, we leave cookies and milk for Santa.

Conclusion

Today we honor St. Nicholas. We celebrate charity, thinking about and giving to others without expecting anything in return. St. Nicholas practiced what Jesus taught.

- That's what St. Nicholas is all about.
- That's what Santa Claus is all about.
- That's what Jesus is all about!

Related Liturgical Suggestions

At the end of the celebration, include a visit from "St. Nick" bearing small gifts for the children.

St. Patrick

Focus Group

Primary/Intermediate Grades

Liturgical/Scriptural References

March 17
Lectionary #541 (#719-724)

Notes

Use a large green shamrock as a prop for this homily.

Situating the Homily

Patrick was a Christian who lived a long time ago in Scotland. At age 16, he was captured by pirates! He was sold as a slave in Ireland (which at that time was a non-Christian country). After several months, he managed to escape and go back home.

Eventually, he decided God wanted him to be a priest and to go back to Ireland as a missionary.

Developing the Main Points

Patrick traveled all over Ireland:

- preaching
- teaching
- establishing schools
- baptizing thousands
- establishing the Catholic church all over Ireland
- sending missionaries to Europe

He did so well that Ireland became known as the "Isle of Saints and Scholars."

Patrick was a man of

- action
- fierce determination
- unrelenting courage

He used the shamrock in his teaching. Some people had difficulty with the idea of the Trinity (one God = three Persons), which can be hard to explain and to understand. The Irish people thought Patrick had had too much Irish coffee! So he used the shamrock, saying:

"The shamrock represents the Trinity. Just as three shamrock leaves are joined onto a single stem, the Trinity is three in one, and God is all of them."

The Irish decided, "Still difficult to understand, but we believe."

Conclusion

Everywhere Patrick went, he planted shamrocks to remind people about the Trinity!

Shamrocks became the symbol of St. Patrick's Day to remind us of how St. Patrick taught about the Trinity.

Related Liturgical Suggestions

Remember St. Patrick's Day occurs during Lent. Don't lose the lenten focus.

Ss. Peter and Paul

Focus Group

Junior High Students

**Liturgical/Scriptural
References**

Feast: June 29
Acts 12:1-11
Jn 21:15-19
Mt 16:13-19

Situating the Homily

Peter and Paul were two men who were different (they sometimes disagreed) yet united in a common purpose: to spread the Good News of Jesus Christ.

Both changed their names

- Simon = Peter
- Saul = Paul

Developing the Main Points

Peter was the leader of the apostles. He was a fisherman. Sometimes he was weak (in fact, he denied Jesus three times) but he always picked himself up and tried over and over again to be faithful and loving.

He became a...

- rock of faith
- rock of strength

- the leader of the early Christian community

Paul was a scholar. At first, he persecuted the early Christians. He was determined and headstrong; eventually, he used these same qualities for the sake of the Gospel. He was always urging people to be more like Jesus, who was with them and in them.

Everyone has different gifts and abilities. Every one of us here is different. We all have gifts; some have the...

- gift of listening
- gift of talking
- gift of efficiency

...and so on.

Conclusion

What special gifts/talents/abilities do you have?

How can you use them for the sake of the Gospel?

Peter and Paul were so different in personality and background yet so similar in their love of Jesus and dedication to Gospel.

We are all different. We come in all sizes and shapes and with different gifts and abilities. But we are united by the Spirit:

- All of us serve the same God.
- All of us can use our unique talents for Jesus!

Related Liturgical Suggestions

Place a picture, icon, or statue of Peter and Paul in the entrance or gathering area.

St. Valentine's Day

Focus Group

Primary Grades

**Liturgical/Scriptural
References**

February 14 (Jn 15:9-17)

Situating the Homily

What is February 14?

Who is St. Valentine

Valentine was an early Christian martyr. Legend has it
that he would send notes of love and encouragement to
other Christians during times of persecution and sign
them "From Your Valentine."

Developing the Main Points

What do we do on St. Valentine's Day? We remember
his love

- for God
- for others

How do we celebrate St. Valentine's Day? We send/give
valentine cards and gifts.

Why? To whom do we give these cards/gifts? What do
they mean?

They are signs of

- love

- friendship

- enjoyment of others

God gives us a valentine, too—one that we get every day: Jesus.

Jesus is God's valentine to us to show us God's

- love

- friendship

- appreciation of us

Conclusion

How does God give us Jesus daily?

- Word

- sacrament

- others (parents, friends, etc.)

- faith community

- inner confidence and strength

Jesus is our daily valentine from God because God cares enough to send the very best!

Related Liturgical Suggestions

In the homily or at the end of Mass, ask everyone to think of one act of love they will perform for someone in the coming week.

Encourage the children to possibly make/send/give a Valentine card to an elderly person, to someone who might be lonely, etc.

28th Sunday of the Year (C)

Focus Group   **Notes**

Intermediate Grades

Liturgical/Scriptural References

Lectionary #145
Adaptable for Thanksgiving Day

Situating the Homily

When you receive a favor or gift, your parents, teachers, and others might often coax you by saying, "What do you say?"

You reply: "Thank you!"

Often, we all have to remind ourselves to say "thank you,"

- remind ourselves to be grateful
- remind ourselves of our duties and obligations to God, others, and self

Developing the Main Points

The Holy Spirit is the Great Reminder.

St. Paul, inspired by the Spirit, reminds us that Jesus is raised from the dead.

The Spirit helps us remember

- to say "thank you" (like the leper in the Gospel)
- how good God is

- Jesus' death and resurrection
- that he is present within and among us
- that we are brothers and sisters

If we remember these things, some things will have to change—*we* will have to change—and become

- more compassionate
- kinder
- more responsive to needs of others

But sometimes—many times—we forget.

Conclusion

The Holy Spirit helps us to

- remember
- refresh
- renew ourselves!

Related Liturgical Suggestions

After the preparation of the gifts and before the preface, point out that the word "Eucharist" is the Greek word for "thank you" or "thanksgiving."

Triumph of the Cross

Focus Group

Junior High Students

Notes

Liturgical/Scriptural References

September 14
Lectionary #638

Situating the Homily

We are surrounded by crosses. We see the cross

- when we make the sign of the cross
- on the walls in church and at home
- on the tops of our churches
- in jewelry: earrings and necklaces

Developing the Main Points

We wear crosses. We bear crosses as well, such as when we experience

- slanders against our reputations (being labelled "easy" or a "nerd")
- abuse
- parental divorce
- loneliness

- alcoholism and other drug addictions
- low grades
- personality problems
- physical or mental handicaps or illnesses
- weight disorders

Everyone has a cross to bear, but Jesus tells us: "Pick up your cross; don't let it crush you!" With Jesus' help, we can

- gain confidence
- move on
- get "unstuck"

Jesus helps us to know that we're not alone; he gives his Holy Spirit to build our

- courage
- compassion
- strength

Holiness means sticking close to Jesus through

- prayer
- sacraments
- self-awareness and self-love

Conclusion

Pick up your cross; don't let it get you down.
Keep following Jesus; keep moving on with Jesus!

Related Liturgical Suggestions

Hand out to everyone an adaptation of the "Order for the Blessing of Religious Articles" from the *Book of Blessings* to take home to bless their household crosses.

 **Vocation**

Focus Group   **Notes**

Intermediate/Junior High

**Liturgical/Scriptural
References**

Mt 9:36-38

Situating the Homily

Look at your hands! What do you see?

- dirt

- ink

- chewed up fingernails

- scars

- traces of breakfast

What are you going to do with your hands for the rest of your life? Will you use them

- to hurt or heal?

- to beat or bless?

- to pull triggers or perform operations?

Developing the Main Points

Look at your parents' hands. Your father's hands might be

- calloused

- big

- affectionate

- rough from hard labor

Your mother's hands might be

- worn

- "dishpan"

- gentle, caressing

- cookie makers!

The important thing is to use your hands for God, to do something beautiful for God. Your parents use their hands for you and for God. You, too, can use your hands for others and for God. In this way, you

- benefit others

- express God's love for everyone and everything

Conclusion

Each of us needs to find the best way we can use our hands for God:

- as a parent

- as a priest, nun, or other religious

- as a single person

- as a friend

Whatever you do, use your hands for God!

Related Liturgical Suggestions

Invite everyone to pray the Lord's Prayer with arms extended and palms upturned as a way of emphasizing their hands.

 **We Are Sent!**

Focus Group   **Notes**

Primary/Intermediate Grades

Liturgical/Scriptural References

Acts 13:4-12

Situating the Homily

Whenever you are sent somewhere, there's a reason:

- You might be sent to the principal's office with a message.

- You might be sent to the store to buy milk or bread.

There's a reason, a purpose, for being sent.

Developing the Main Points

For example, Paul and Barnabas were sent to Salamis to preach the Good News of Jesus—that was the purpose of their mission, of their "being sent."

Jesus was sent to tell/show us what God the Father wanted us to know/do.

We too are sent

- because of our baptism

- because we are Christian

But to where? Why are we sent?

To spread the Good News!

What are the last words we hear at Mass?

"Go in peace to love and serve the Lord."

We are commissioned. Our attention is directed to the job ahead of us:

- be a friend
- praise and thank God
- work for God's kingdom

Conclusion

Remember, we are sent!

Related Liturgical Suggestions

For the final blessing, use the "Order of Blessing of Missionaries" from the *Book of Blessings*.

Bibliography

Required Reading

Coles, Robert. *The Spiritual Life of Children*. Boston: Houghton Mifflin Company, 1990.

Directory for Masses with Children. In *The Liturgy Documents: A Parish Resource*. 3rd ed. Chicago: Liturgy Training Publications, 1991.

"Eucharistic Prayers for Children." *Sacramentary*. New York: Catholic Book Publishing Co., 1985.

Introduction to *Lectionary for Masses with Children*. 3 vols. (cycles A,B,C). San Jose: Resource Publications, Inc. 1993-94.

Jeep, Elizabeth McMahon, et al. *The Welcome Table*. Chicago: Liturgy Training Publications, 1982.

Miffleton, Jack. *Sunday's Child*. Washington, DC: The Pastoral Press, 1989.

Homiletics

Baker, Brant D. *Let the Children Come*. Minneapolis: Augsburg, 1991.

Brennan-Nichols, Patricia. *Liturgies & Lessons: Children's Homilies*. Lake Worth, Florida: Sunday Publications, Inc., 1984.

Coleman, Richard. *Gospel-Telling: The Art and Theology of Children's Sermons*. Grand Rapids: Wm. B. Eerdmans Publishing Co., 1982.

Cronin, Gaynell. *Sunday Throughout the Week*. Notre Dame: Ave Maria Press, 1981.

Cronin, Gaynell Bordes. *Holy Days & Holidays*. 2 vols. San Francisco: Harper & Row, Publishers, 1979-88.

Jordan, Jerry Marshall. *The Brown Bag*. New York: Pilgrim Press, 1978.

———. *Another Brown Bag*. New York: Pilgrim Press, 1980.

———. *Filling Up the Brown Bag*. New York: Pilgrim Press, 1987.

Pottebaum, Gerard A. *To Walk with a Child*. Loveland, Ohio: Treehaus Communications, Inc., 1993.

Shaughnessy, Anne Hirsch. *God's Word for Little Ones*. Notre Dame: Ave Maria Press, 1991.

Wharton, Paul J. *Stories and Parables for Preachers and Teachers*. New York: Paulist Press, 1986.

Christian Folk Stories

Juknialis, Joseph J. *Angels to Wish By: A Book of Story-Prayers*. San Jose: Resource Publications, Inc., 1983.

————. *A Stillness Without Shadows*. San Jose: Resource Publications, Inc., 1986.

————. *When God Began in the Middle*. San Jose: Resource Publication, Inc., 1982.

————. *Winter Dreams and Other Such Friendly Dragons*. San Jose: Resource Publications, Inc., 1979.

Saints

Celebrating the Saints. New York: Pueblo Publishing Company, 1978.

Foley, Leonard, ed. *Saint of the Day*. Cincinnati: St. Anthony Messenger Press, 1990.

Marbach, Ethel Pochocki. *Saints of the Seasons for Children*. Cincinnati: St. Anthony Messenger Press, 1989.

Newland, Mary Reed. *The Saint Book*. San Francisco: Harper & Row, Publishers, 1979.

Yost, Charles E. *In His Likeness*. Hales Corners, Wisconsin: Sacred Heart Monastery, 1988.

Children's Liturgy of the Word

Pottebaum, Gerard A., Sr. Paule Freeburg, DC, and Joyce M. Kelleher. *A Child Shall Lead Them*. Loveland, Ohio: Treehaus Communications, Inc., 1992.

Berglund, Mary Catherine. *Gather the Children: Celebrate the Word*. 3 vols. (cycles A,B,C). Washington, DC: The Pastoral Press, 1989.

Boughton, John and Jill. *Liturgy of the Word for Children*. 3 vols. Northport, New York: Costello Publishing Company, 1988.

Moffatt, Marjorie, SNJM. *Children's Word Liturgies.* 3 vols. Collegeville, Minnesota: The Liturgical Press, 1989.

Stadler, Bernice. *Celebrations of the Word for Children* . 3 vols. Mystic, Connecticut: Twenty-Third Publications, 1986.

Index of Homilies Based on the Liturgical Year

Index of Homilies Based on Sacramental Themes

Index of Homilies Based on Saints' Days

Index of Homilies Based
on Scripture References

More Resources for Working with Children

SUNDAY'S CHILDREN: Prayers in the Language of Children

James Bitney & Suzanne Schaffhausen

Cloth, 80 pages, 6" x 9", ISBN 0-89390-076-1

These children's prayers are ideal both in the classroom and in the home. The authors wrote these prayers to give children a feel for talking to God naturally, which encourages their own spontaneous prayer. A great resource for teachers, librarians, and parents.

GUIDED MEDITATIONS FOR CHILDREN:
40 Scripts and Activities Based on the Sundy Lectionary

Sydney Ann Merritt

Paper, 192 pages, 5½" x 8½", 0-89390-336-1

These guided meditations, related to the Sunday lectionary, include accompanying prayers, discussion questions, and related activities. The book includes tips on how to do guided meditations that work every time. Pick the one you want, adapt it, or read it as is. Great for Children's Liturgy of the Word or for regular catechetical use.

HOW TO PLAN CHILDREN'S LITURGIES

Mary K. Machado

Paper, 96 pages, 6" x 9", 0-89390-074-5

Within this guide, teachers will find valuable techniques for bringing the Mass successfully to children, including a step-by-step outline to plan liturgies, a proposed method for developing the prayer expression of children, and a procedure to help children participate in liturgies.

Call 1-800-736-7600 for current prices.
See next page for order information.

Resources for Children's Liturgy of the Word

CHILDREN'S LITURGY OF THE WORD
from CELEBRATING THE LECTIONARY

Several authors, edited by Liz Montes

Looseleaf, 347 pages, 8½" x 11"
Published annually in August

If you dismiss children for a separate Children's Liturgy of the Word, this is the packet for you. This liturgical packet contains background on planning liturgies for children, commentary on the seasons and on each Sunday's readings, a service plan for each Sunday, and tips for proclamation, as well as homilies for children. This packet covers every Sunday of the year starting with the first Sunday in September.

LECTIONARY FOR MASSES WITH CHILDREN

Three volumes (cycles A, B, C), cloth, 640 pages, 8½" x 11"

This Lectionary is intended to help those ministering to children. Use this lectionary for Children's Liturgy of the Word and Masses with children. It contains readings for the Sundays of the cycle and weekdays. Approved for use in the United States by the National Conference of Catholic Bishops.

Order from your local bookseller, or call toll-free 1-800-736-7600, fax 1-408-287-8748, or write to:

 Resource Publications, Inc.
160 E. Virginia Street #290-OQ
San Jose, CA 95112-5876